SCHIRMER'S LIBRARY
OF MUSICAL CLASSICS

Vol. 221

JOHANN SEBASTIAN BACH

Sonatas and Partitas

For Violin Solo

Edited by

EDUARD HERRMANN

G. SCHIRMER, Inc.

DISTRIBUTED BY

HAL•LEONARD®
CORPORATION

7777 W. BLUEMOUND RD. P.O. BOX 13819 MILWAUKEE, WI 53213

PREFACE.

JOHANN SEBASTIAN BACH, one of the greatest German musicians, was born in 1685, and died in 1750. His works are monuments of his art, unsurpassed masterworks in Counterpoint, Polyphony and Harmony, which not only merit general admiration, but also urge to ardent study ; for it may well be said that Bach's compositions mark an era in the development of modern music.

Among them, the six Sonatas for Violin alone (or, to be more accurate, 3 Partitas and 3 Sonatas), take a prominent place, for in the whole literature of the violin we do not find anything resembling them. It has often been wondered at, how an artist, whose principal instrument was the organ, could have written compositions for the violin which are so extremely difficult, and, at the same time, highly adapted to that instrument. But Bach was an excellent violinist himself. In 1703 he held a position as such in the orchestra of Prince Johann Ernst of Saxe-Weimar, and the six Sonatas were probably written during that time.

In publishing this new edition, it was my endeavor to keep strictly in accord with the original ; not to modernize the expression, not to change the underlying harmony, and as little as possible the bowings and signs, for only in this way can we get a true picture of Bach's intellectual greatness. In the celebrated Ciaconna, for instance, trills had to be omitted, chords completed, runs harmonically changed, the duration of notes prolonged, etc. All this may sound strange to those who do not know the original, but it is in exact correspondence with the manuscript on which the edition of the "Bach-Gesellschaft" is based.

With regard to the signs, a few explanations are necessary. The metronome ought not to be used for more than a few measures ; the *spiccato* bowing is indicated by dots (......), the legato by lines (— — — —) or not at all. The *ritardandos* at the close of a part are not to be observed when that part is repeated.

In conclusion, I dedicate this new edition to my friend, Mr. Maurice Sternberger, and to all sincere students who find an inexhaustible source of inspiration and enjoyment in the works of our great master, J. S. Bach.

EDUARD HERRMANN.

Sonata No. 1 in G minor

BWV 1001

4

Fuga.
Allegro. ($\bullet$ = 72)

6

Siciliano. (Old quiet dance of a pastoral character.)

Andante. (♪ = 88)

8

Presto. (♩.= 72)

Partita No. 1 in B minor
BWV 1002

Allemanda (German dance of moderate movement.)

Double. (Varied and embellished repetitions of a theme.)

Corrente. (Old dance of a vivacious character.)

Double.
Presto. ($\boldsymbol{\downarrow}$ = 100)

Sarabande. (Old Spanish dance of a grave character.)

Double.

Bourrée. (Old French dance in lively motion.)

Tempo di Bourrée. (♩=69)

Double.

$(\text{♩} = 92)$

Sonata No. 2 in A minor
BWV 1003

Grave
(M. M. ♪ = 52)

Fuga.
($\quad = 76$)

cresc. poco a poco

mp

cresc. poco a poco

cresc.

cresc.

dim.

pesante

lento
rit. cresc.
ff

Andante.

(♪ = 60) The lower notes must be held as long as possible.

Allegro.
($\bullet$ = 80)

Partita No. 2 in D minor
BWV 1004

Allemanda
(M.M. ♩ = 76)

Corrente.
(♩= 88)

Sarabanda.
($\bullet$ = 58)

Giga. (An old quick dance)

(♩. = 72)

Ciaccona. (A slow piece of not more than eight measures, with manifold variations.)

Sonata No. 3 in C Major
BWV 1005

Fuga.
Alla breve. ($\stackrel{|}{\downarrow}$ = 66)

mf

dim.

p

f

p

p

mf

f

ff

p

tr

p

poco a poco cresc.

47

Largo.
Con espressione. (♪ = 69)

Allegro assai. ($\bullet$ = 96)

Partita No. 3 in E Major
BWV 1006

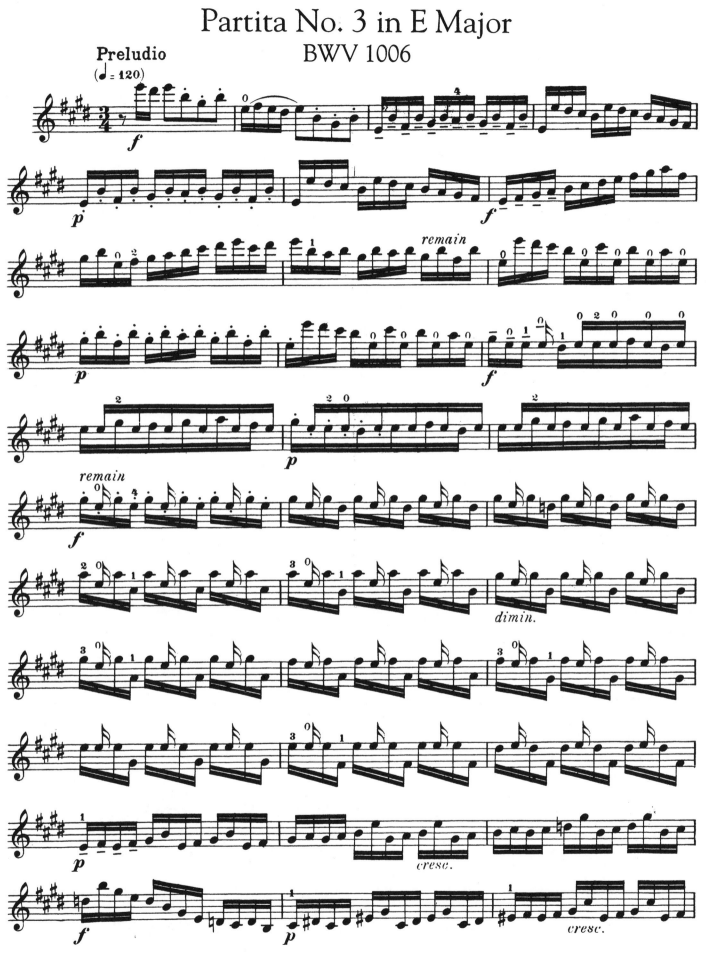

Loure. (A dance of moderate movement.)

Gavotte en Rondeau. (An old French dance in Rondoform.)

Menuetto I. (A French dance of very moderate movement.)

Menuetto II.

Bourrée. A gay and lively dance, which originated in Auvergne (France).

Giga. (An old and very fast dance.)
($\quad$ = 69.)